BRJC
7/2014

TULSA CITY-COUNTY LIBRARY

D1257825

Measurement

in

tsp

BY SARA PISTOIA

The Child's World

Published by The Child's World®
1980 Lookout Drive • Mankato, MN 56003-1705
800-599-READ • www.childsworld.com

Acknowledgments
The Child's World®: Mary Berendes, Publishing Director
The Design Lab: Design
Editing: Jody Jensen Shaffer

Photographs ©: BrandXPictures: 10; PhotoDisc: 6, 22;
all other photographs David M. Budd Photography.

Copyright © 2014 by The Child's World®
All rights reserved. No part of this book may be reproduced or utilized in
any form or by any means without written permission from the publisher.

ISBN 9781623235314
LCCN 2013931391

Printed in the United States of America
Mankato, MN
July, 2013
PA02173

ABOUT THE AUTHOR

Sara Pistoia is a retired elementary teacher living in Southern California with her husband and a variety of pets. In authoring this series, she draws on the experience of many years of teaching first and second graders.

Measurement

We **measure** things to find out how big they are. We can measure almost anything.

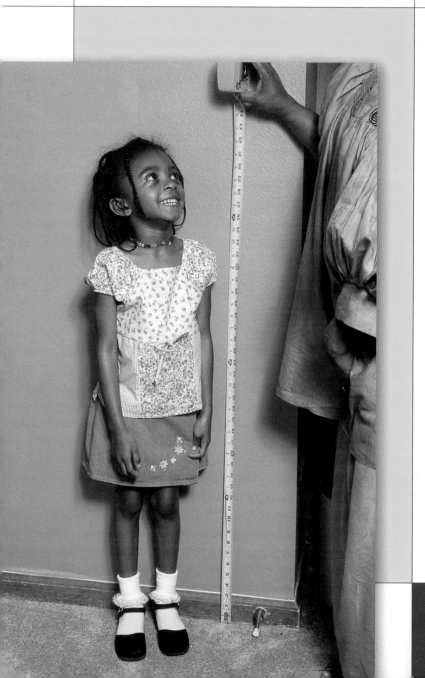

How tall are you? How much does your dog **weigh**? How much milk do you want?

You can measure all these things!

5

We can use simple things to measure. We can use our hands. We can use a cup. We can even use a paperclip!

Each of these things can be a **unit of measure**.

You always need to say which unit of measure you are using.

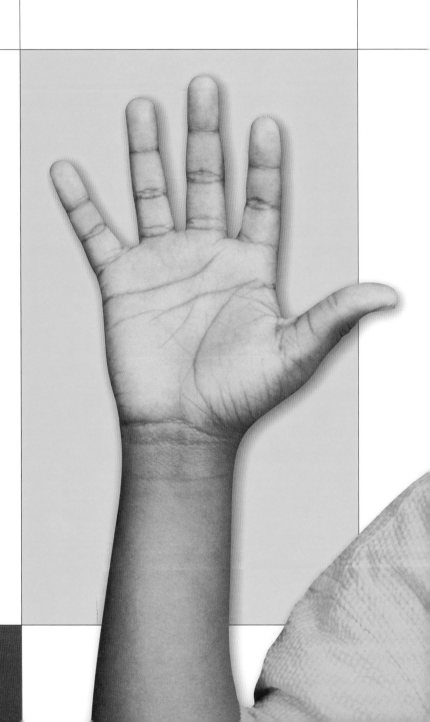

Let's measure a carrot.

This carrot is about seven long.

Seven *what* long?

This carrot is about seven paperclips long.

Let's measure some water.

This bucket holds ten.

Ten *what*?

Ten teacups of water!

Now measure a desk with your hands. Did you measure about six or seven hands wide? Did you measure about ten hands long?

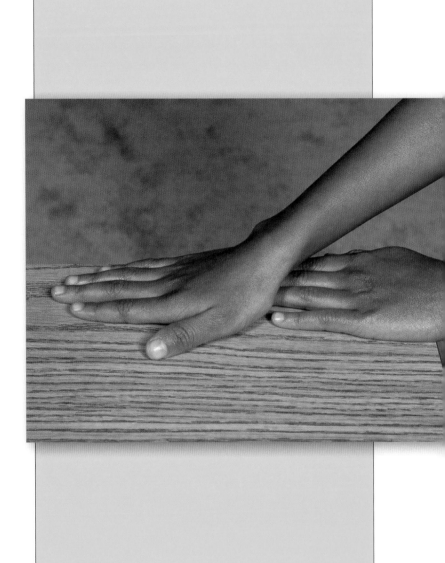

Find a grown-up to measure the desk.

A grown-up's hands are bigger than your hands. With their hands, the desk is only four hands wide.

We need units of measure that do not change when different people use them.

We need units of measure that are the same for everyone. We need measuring tools.

How many of the tools on page 11 can you find at home or at school?

Everyone can use the tools shown here, and the measurements will stay the same!

Did you find a **ruler**? This ruler measures in units called **inches**. Let's measure the carrot again! The ruler says the carrot is eight inches long.

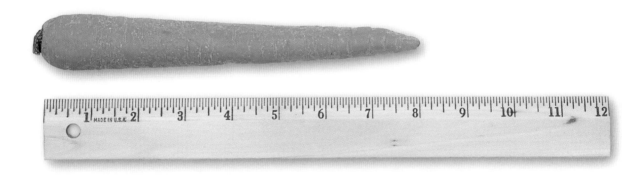

A ruler is twelve inches long. Twelve inches equals one **foot**. A foot is another unit of measure.

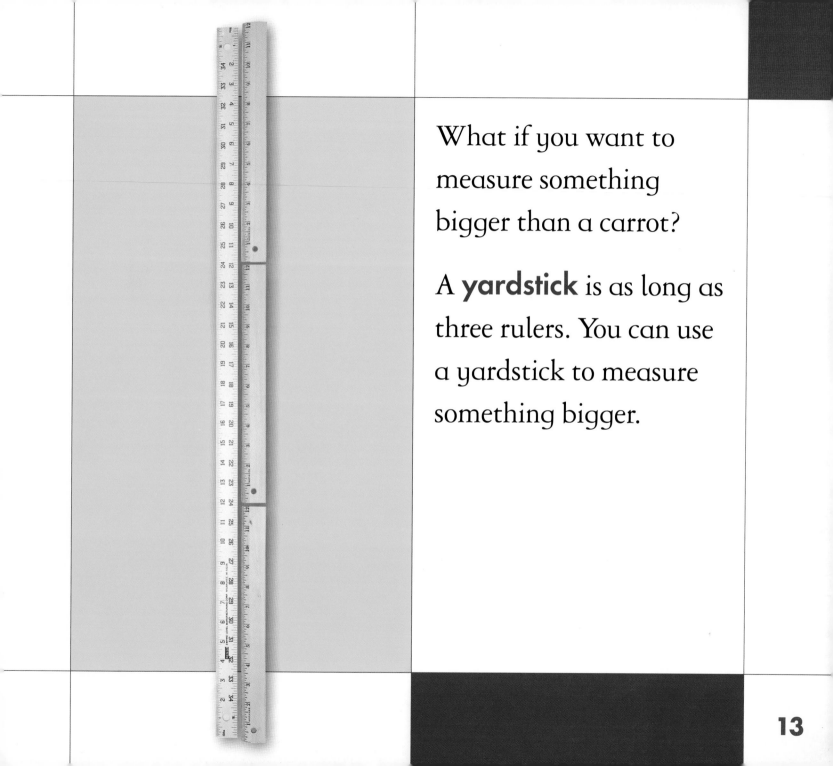

What if you want to measure something bigger than a carrot?

A **yardstick** is as long as three rulers. You can use a yardstick to measure something bigger.

Now measure the desk with a yardstick. Ask a grown-up to measure it, too.

You agree! The desk is eighteen inches wide.

Choose the best tool to measure things. Use a ruler for small things. Use a yardstick for big things.

Would you use a ruler or a yardstick to measure a candy bar?

A flag?

We can measure this teddy bear in inches. It is taller than the twelve-inch ruler. The bear is about fourteen inches tall.

But how big is the teddy bear's head? You can use a **tape measure** to find out. It can go around the teddy bear's head.

A tape measure can measure things that are round.

17

Do you want to know how heavy something is? You can't use a ruler. You can't use a tape measure.

You can use a **scale**! You can find a scale at a grocery store. Many foods are measured in **ounces** or **pounds**.

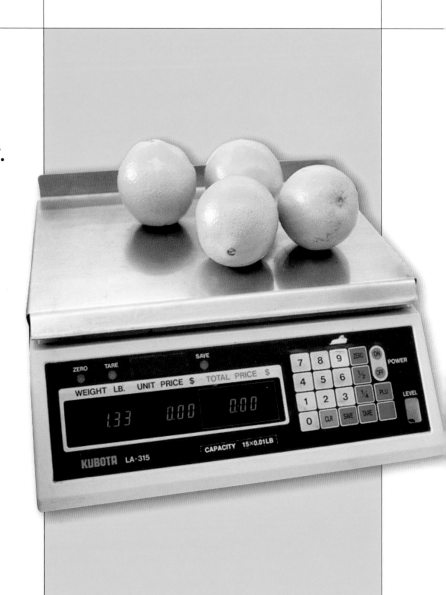

You can measure your dog on a scale, too. Wow! This dog weighs 102 pounds!

Wet things like milk or water are called **liquids**. How do you measure liquids?

Dry things like sugar and cereal are called **solids**. How do you measure solids?

Do you want to make some cookies? Use these tools to measure the foods you'll need!

There are other units of measure for food, too.

You can buy a **gallon** of milk.

You can buy a **cup** of yogurt.

You can buy a **quart** of ice cream.

There are so many things to measure!

How tall are you?

How much do you weigh?

How much ice cream can you eat?

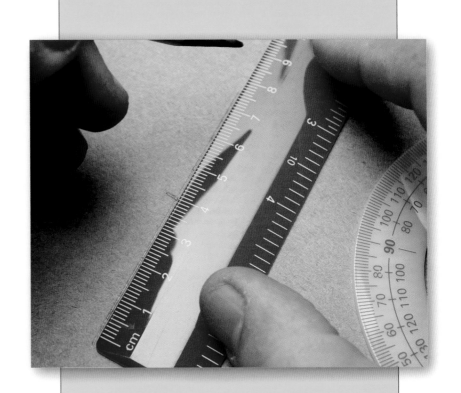

Just remember: choose the right tool when you measure something. It makes the job as easy as one, two, three!

23

Key Words

cup
foot
gallon
inches
liquids
measure
ounces
pounds
quart
ruler
scale
solids
tape measure
unit of measure
weigh
yardstick

Index